W9-CDD-411

WITHDRAWN

MAPS

Pebble® Plus

Compass Roses and Directions

by
Jennifer M. Besel

Consulting editor:
Gail Saunders-Smith, PhD

Consultant:
Dr. Sarah E. Battersby
Department of Geography
University of South Carolina

CAPSTONE PRESS
a capstone imprint

Pebble Plus is published by Capstone Press,
1710 Roe Crest Drive, North Mankato, Minnesota 56003
www.capstonepub.com

Copyright © 2014 by Capstone Press, a Capstone imprint. All rights reserved. No part of this publication may be reproduced in whole or in part, or stored in a retrieval system, or transmitted in any form or by any means, electronic, mechanical, photocopying, recording, or otherwise, without written permission of the publisher.

Library of Congress Cataloging-in-Publication Data
Besel, Jennifer M.
Compass roses and directions / by Jennifer M. Besel.
p. cm.—(Pebble plus. Maps)
Includes bibliographical references and index.
Summary: "Simple text with full-color photos and illustrations provide basic information about compass roses and map directions"—Provided by publisher.
ISBN 978-1-4765-3084-0 (library binding)—ISBN 978-1-4765-3506-7 (ebook pdf)—ISBN 978-1-4765-3524-1 (paperback)
1. Cardinal points—Juvenile literature. 2. Maps—Symbols—Juvenile literature. I. Title.
G108.5.C3B47 2014
912.01'48—dc23   2012046449

Editorial Credits
Gene Bentdahl, designer; Kathy McColley, production specialist; Sarah Schuette, photo stylist; Marcy Morin, scheduler

Photo Credits
Capstone: 7, 9 (front); Capstone Studio: Karon Dubke, cover, 1, 5, 9 (back), 11, 13, 15, 17, 19, 21

Note to Parents and Teachers

The Maps set supports social studies standards related to people, places, and environments. This book describes and illustrates compass roses and map directions. The images support early readers in understanding the text. The repetition of words and phrases helps early readers learn new words. This book also introduces early readers to subject-specific vocabulary words, which are defined in the Glossary section. Early readers may need assistance to read some words and to use the Table of Contents, Glossary, Read More, Internet Sites, and Index sections of the book.

Printed in the United States of America in North Mankato, Minnesota.
032013   007223CGF13

Table of Contents

Which Way?

Have you ever been lost?

A map is a great tool

to help you find your way.

On a map you can see

roads or buildings.

Maps show which direction

one place is from another.

Island Pond, Vermont

Key

Store

Library

Church

House

0   50 feet

15 meters

Walnut Avenue

Middle Street

North Street

N
W   E
S

Getting Directions

Maps use cardinal directions
to show the way.
Cardinal directions are north,
south, east, and west.

North

West ←→ East

South

Village ■ ■ Fishing Bridge

The compass rose shows
which way is north, south,
east, or west on the map.

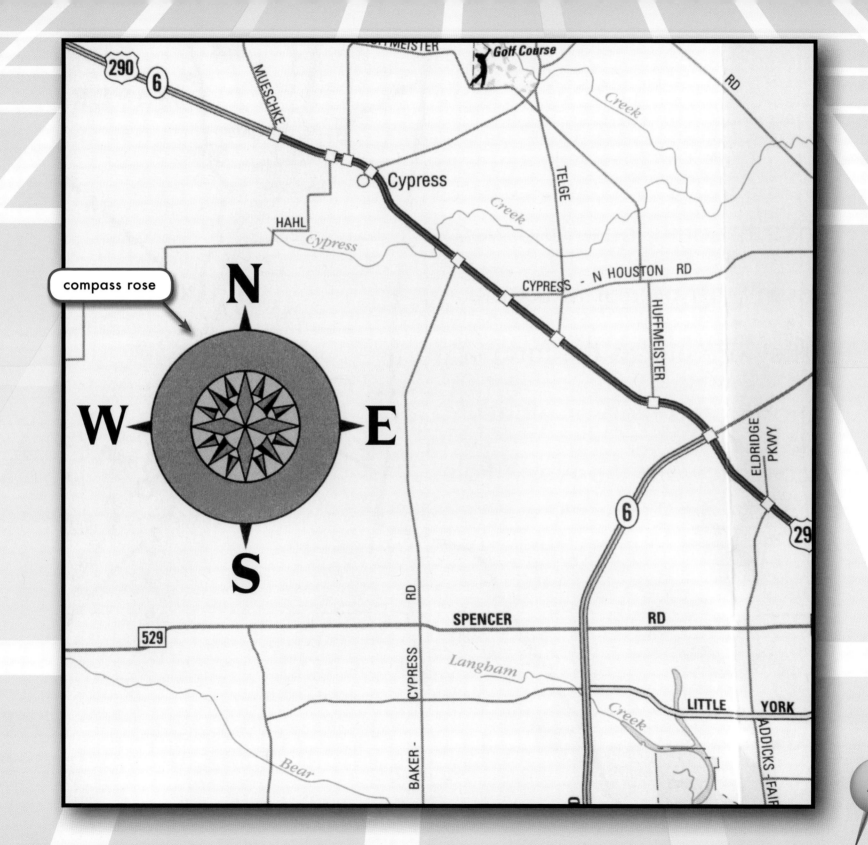

compass rose

North, south, east, and west

aren't just points on a map.

They are places on Earth.

North on a map or globe

points toward the North Pole.

3 1889 00360 4898

13

Compasses

A compass shows

where north is on Earth.

A compass needle

always points

toward the North Pole.

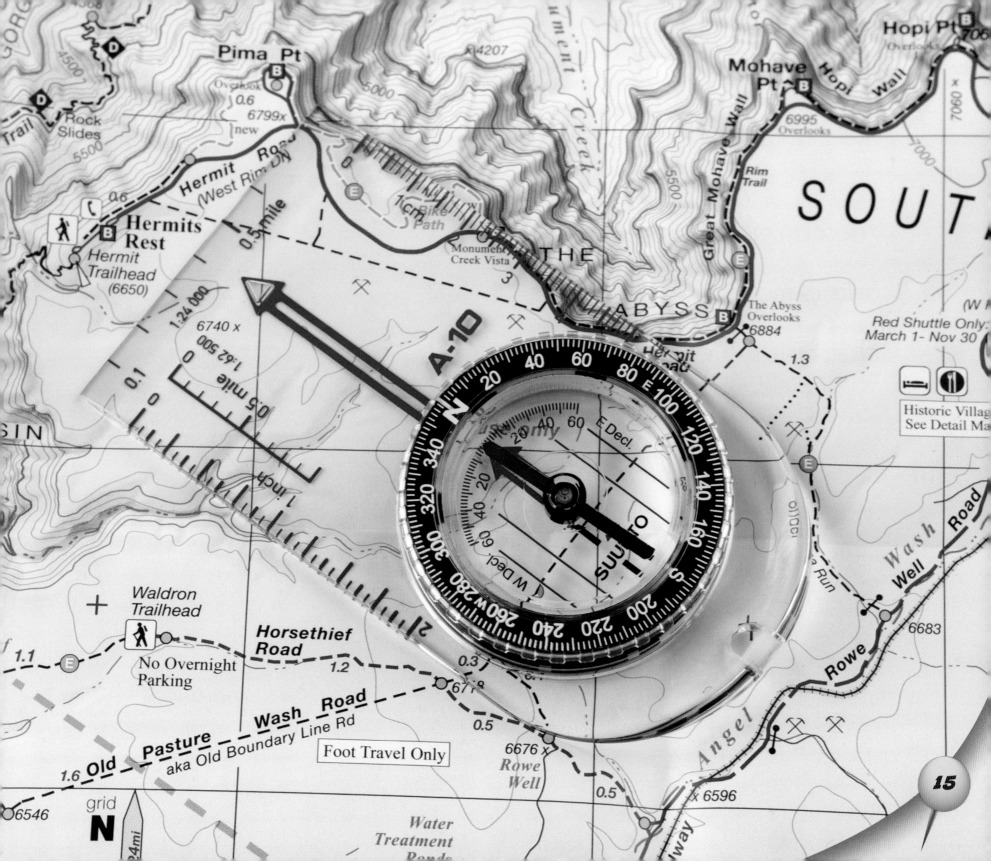

Using Map Tools

You can use a compass
and a map to travel.
First, use the compass
to find north on Earth.

Next, turn your map

so north on the compass rose

points to Earth's north.

Follow the map

to get where you're going!

Glossary

cardinal direction—one of the four main points toward which something can face; north, south, east, and west

compass—an instrument used for finding directions

compass rose—a label that shows direction on a map

globe—a round model of the world

North Pole—the most northern point on Earth

Read More

Besel, Jennifer M. *Types of Maps.* Maps. North Mankato, Minn.: Capstone Press, 2014.

Cunningham, Kevin. *Types of Maps.* A True Book. New York: Children's Press, 2013.

Spilsbury, Louise. *Mapping.* Investigate. Chicago: Heinemann Library, 2010.

Internet Sites

FactHound offers a safe, fun way to find Internet sites related to this book. All of the sites on FactHound have been researched by our staff.

Here's all you do:

Visit *www.facthound.com*

Type in this code: 9781476530840

Check out projects, games and lots more at
www.capstonekids.com

Critical Thinking Using the Common Core

1. What is the role of a compass rose? (Key Ideas and Details)

2. Describe the steps to use a map and compass together. (Key Ideas and Details)

3. Look at the photograph and map on page 9. If the children are at the village, which direction should they go to reach the fishing bridge? Describe how you reached your answer. (Craft and Structure)

Index

Word Count: 151
Grade: 1
Early-Intervention Level: 17